This coloring book represents just a handful of the hundreds of distinctive architectural drawings of Allentown, Pennsylvania area buildings that Leah Anderson has produced over the years, making her one of the better known artists in the Lehigh Valley area.

Leah's talents are not; however, confined to only this particular type of art. She is the owner and operator of Leah's . . . The Gallery, a full-service art gallery and custom framing service at 512 Hamilton Street, Allentown. In addition, she has received numerous awards and citations for her oil paintings and pencil drawings. The Allentown Downtown Improvement District commissioned her in 1989 to produce the official Allentown Christmas Card.

In reflecting on her art and her city, Leah says: ''I draw and paint my immediate surroundings because I truly see the beauty of this historic city. With so many East Coast cities having lost their grandeur, it pleases me to live in Allentown where we appreciate our inner city and are doing what we have to in order to preserve it. When I look at the downtown area, I see the soul of the entire city—a soul that deserves all the love and respect we can give it.''

Dedication

This book is dedicated to my Grandfather, John Adolfus Anderson, a gentle giant and an artist who taught me two things: How to draw and how to dream. I could never have done one without the other.

I also want to thank my brother, John Malcolm Anderson, for his help in editing this book.

Trout Hall, Fourth and Linden Streets

Now part of the Lehigh County Historical Society, this mansion was built in 1770 by James Allen, son of the city's founder, William Allen. Several generations of the Allen family lived in this natural stone building. Today it has been remarkably preserved with authentic period furniture and is open for tours.

The Old Lehigh County Courthouse, Fifth and Hamilton Streets

Built between 1814 and 1817, this stately building was a center of judicial, political and religious activities for close to 150 years. Over the years, it has seen such distinguished luminaries as P.T. Barnum, Mark Twain and Horace Greeley use it as a lecture hall. Today it is home to the Lehigh Valley Historical Society as well as the Federal Courts. The new courthouse for Lehigh County was built across the street from this structure in 1961.

The Reichard/Lichtenwalner Farm House, 25th and Tilghman Streets.

This study in the grace of simplicity was built in 1840 as the main residence of one of the city's earliest farms. It has been restored, and today is used as a family residence.

7th Street Brownstone

With its distinctive stone work and round turrets, this brownstone stands out as one of the beautiful in Allentown. It was constructed in the mid 1800s as a summer house for the first president of the Central Railroad of New Jersey. From the turn of the century to 1945, it was the home and office of a well known Allentown physician. Today, it houses several apartments and a photographer's studio.

Symphony Hall, North Sixth Street

Built in 1899 as the Lyric Theater, this building stands as an example of fine architectural detail in a relatively compact space. Not only was it home to countless vaudeville and dramatic theater presentations, it also played a minor role in the famous Broadway play ''42nd Street.'' In that show, the part originally played by Ruby Keeler is that of a young dancer who came from Allentown and got her start at the Lyric Theater. Today, it is the home of the Allentown Symphony.

Antique Car Museum, Fourth and Linden Streets

These two beautiful stone homes were built in the heart of Allentown around 1850. Today, one is used for apartments; the other for an Antique Car Museum.

Carriage House, Ninth and Turner Streets

This colorful and well restored row has a carriage house at one end. Typica

19th century urban living, the carriage house is now used as a bistro.

Allentown Railroad Terminal, Race and Hamilton Streets

Once a passenger station on the Central Railroad of New Jersey line, this stately old building is now a popular restaurant and night spot.

1981 Mayors Award Winner, Sixth and Tilghman Streets

This beautiful mansion stands as a reminder of what hard work and vision can accomplish. After falling into disrepair in the 1960s and 70s, it was purchased in 1979 by a young couple who dedicated themselves to restoring its lustre and bringing forth the incredible amount of architectural detail both inside and out. The porches and wood trims are painted various shades of blue, green and yellow. In 1981, it won the Mayors Award for the best restored home of the year.

Ripensell's Cafe, Eighth and Linden Streets

For over 100 years, this building housed a hotel and bar in the heart of old Allentown. By the 1960s, it had become run down. A group of investors subsequently purchased and restored it, according to preservation guidelines to its current beautiful condition.

The End of a Row, Allen and Law Streets

This beautiful row home is indicative of the contribution made to local Allentown architecture by the Pennsylvania Dutch. Each builder put his own designs over the doors and windows as a signature touch. This particular row home is located on the property of the Old Allentown Fairgrounds Association.

Twin Turret, 12th and Court Streets

This study in achieving elegance through simplicity of design, is fairly typical of many of Allentown's row homes.

A Tree Grows in Allentown, Near North Sixth and Gordon Streets

This particular row of homes is set off from its neighbors by the colorful woodwork and newly planted trees.

Brownstone, North Seventh Street

Now an office for lawyers and other professionals, this graceful mansion was home to one of Allentown's luminaries of the 19th century. Its restored state is proof of the saying: ''Allentown has pride in the past and faith in the future.''